597
Wun

Wu, Norbert

Fish faces

FISH FACES

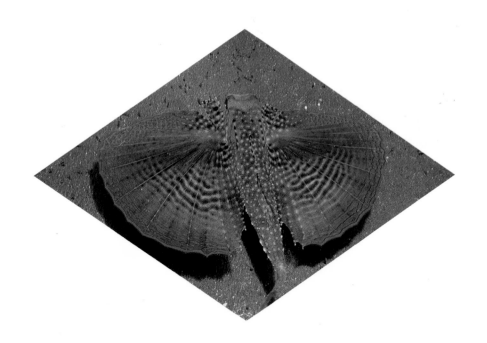

*To Howard Hall, Mark Conlin, Bob Cranston,
and Marty Snyderman, for the good times*

Acknowledgments

My sincere thanks go to Dr. Richard Rosenblatt, H. J. Walker, Cindy Klepallo, and Ken Smith at Scripps Institution of Oceanography for teaching me all I know about ichthyology. The following individuals and organizations provided me with access to the world's best diving: Dive Taveuni and the *Pacific Nomad* in Fiji, the Seychelles Ministry of Tourism, David and Glynnis Rowat at the Seychelles Underwater Center, Samson Shak and Ron Holland of Borneo Divers, Luchi de la Cruz, Tim Sevilla, and Karina Escudero of Divemate Philippines, and Gwen Roland at *Scuba Times* magazine. Dan Walsh, Dan Auber, Brandon Cole, Burt Jones, Randall Kosaki, Jackie Young, and James Watt have been great buddies, both underwater and above. Further thanks go to Adrienne Betz and Simone Kaplan, my editors, who supported my ideas and helped organize them into this book.

Henry Holt and Company, Inc., *Publishers since 1866*
115 West 18th Street, New York, New York 10011

Henry Holt is a registered trademark of Henry Holt and Company, Inc.

Published in Canada by Fitzhenry & Whiteside Ltd.,
195 Allstate Parkway, Markham, Ontario L3R 4T8.

Library of Congress Cataloging-in-Publication Data
Wu, Norbert. Fish faces / Norbert Wu.
Summary: The author-photographer, a marine biologist, uses his own
photographs to introduce readers to some of the more amusing
characteristics of the creatures he's encountered on his dives.
1. Fishes—Juvenile literature. [1. Fishes. 2. Marine biology.]
I. Title. QL617.2.W82 1993   597—dc20   92-27343

ISBN 0-8050-1668-6 (hardcover)
1 3 5 7 9 10 8 6 4 2
ISBN 0-8050-5347-6 (paperback)
1 3 5 7 9 10 8 6 4 2

Published in hardcover in 1993 by Henry Holt and Company, Inc.
First Owlet paperback edition, 1997

Printed in the United States of America on acid-free paper. ∞

FISH FACES

NORBERT WU

Henry Holt and Company ◆ **New York**

One fish, two fish, three fish, more
Fish that dart and dip and slide

Fish that glide on fins like wings

Flat fish, round fish
A very long and thin fish

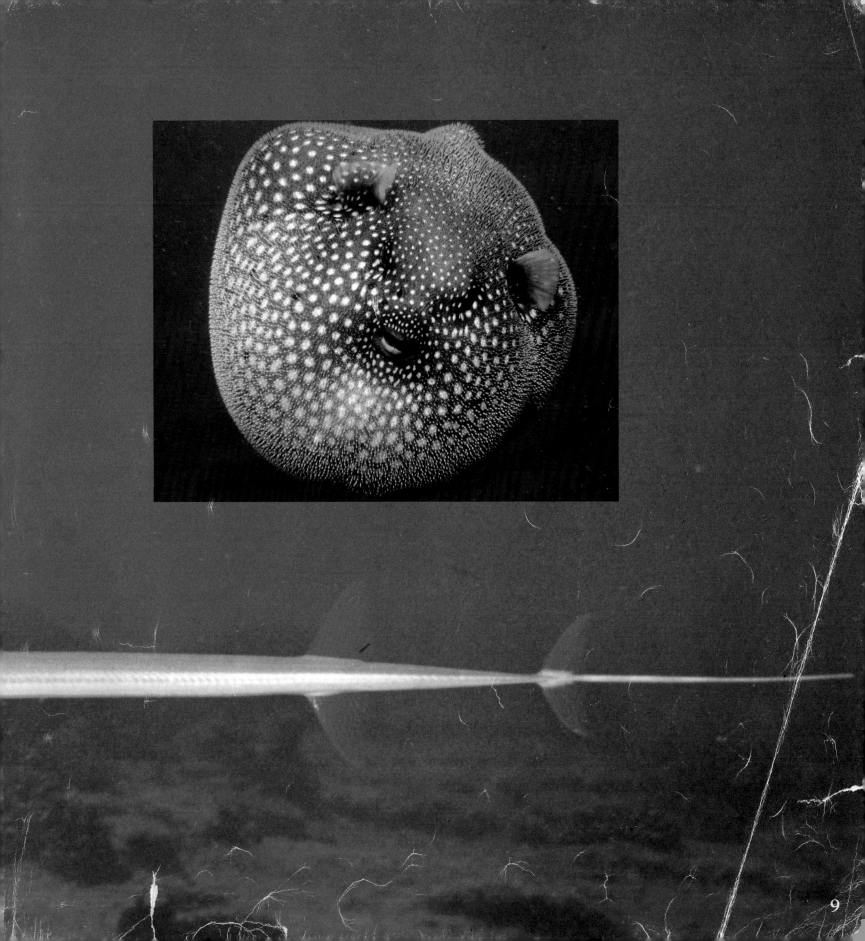

Spotted fish, dotted fish

Fish with lines and stripes and waves

Fish with spikes and spines and branches

14

Fish with mouths that open wide
Mouth like a tube, mouth like a beak
Mouth that belongs to a monster of the deep

A long nose, a flat nose, a hard-to-ignore nose
A nose that looks like it could cut wood
A nose that shines in the dark!

Red eyes

Green eyes

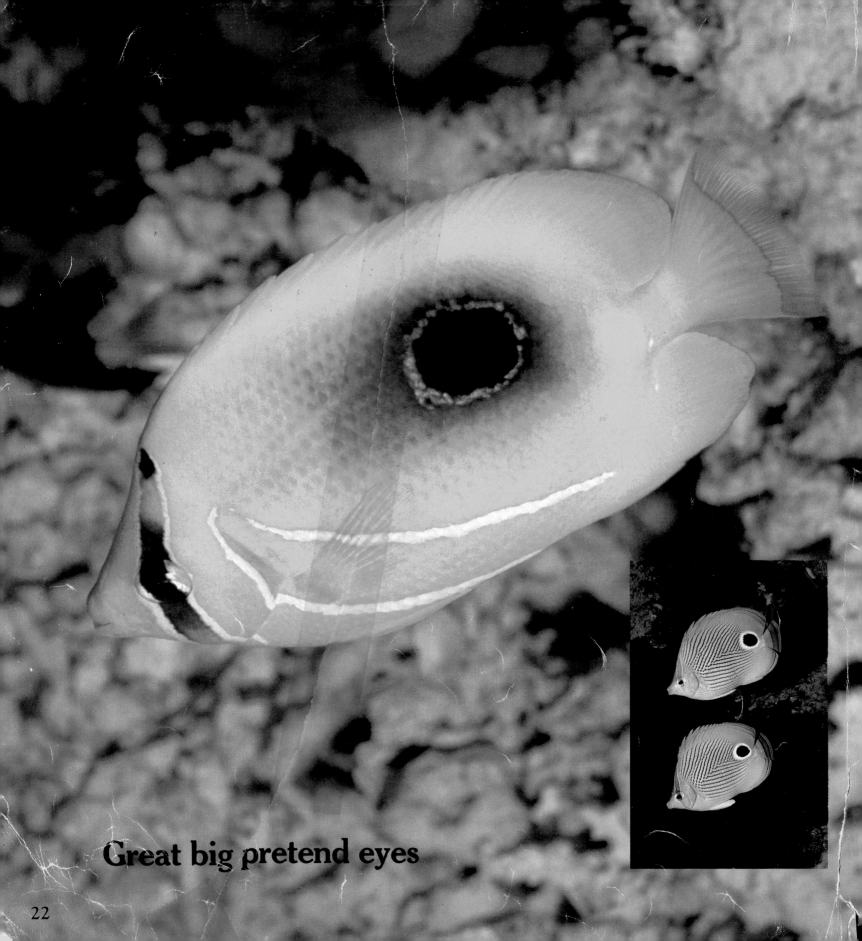

Great big pretend eyes

Eyes that are hooded

Eyes that shine

Eyes that stick up like periscopes

Faces that are friendly

Faces that are fierce

Faces that could be sad or mad

28

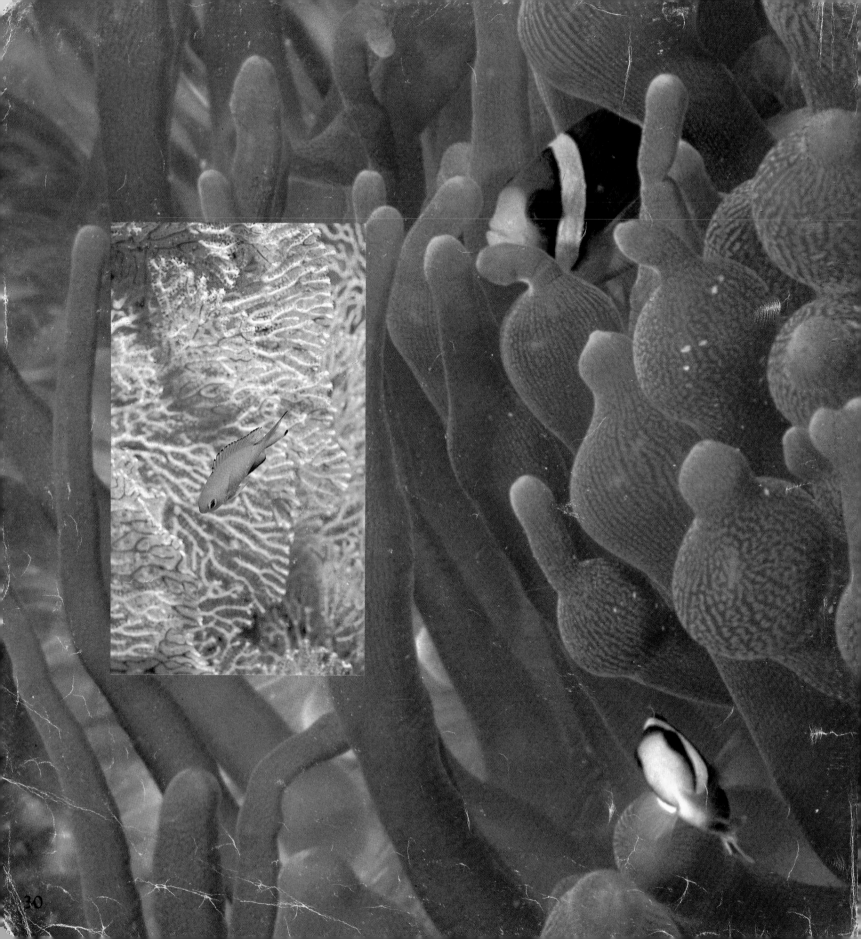

One fish, two fish, three fish, four
Deep in the ocean, there are thousands more!

NOTES

There are thousands of different fish in the ocean.
Here are the names of those that appear in this book:

Front Cover
Clown anemonefish

Back Cover
Inflated porcupinefish

Half title
Flying gurnard

Title page
Clockwise from top left: larval fangtooth;
anemonefish; whitemouth moray eel

Pages 4 and 5
Left to right: garibaldi; anemonefish; sergeant
majors. Inset: king angelfish

Pages 6 and 7
Background: bat rays
Insets left to right: flying gurnard; flying fish;
southern stingray; Pacific angel shark.

Pages 8 and 9
Background: cornetfish
Insets left to right: peacock flounder; big skate;
inflated guineafowl puffer.

Pages 10 and 11
Background: blue-spotted jawfish
Page 10 Insets top to bottom: blue-spotted
stingray; guineafowl puffer; coral grouper
Page 11 Insets top to bottom: whitemouth moray
eel; scrawled filefish; clown triggerfish

Pages 12 and 13
Background: anemonefish. Clockwise from top left:
king angelfish; regal angelfish; harlequin tuskfish;
clown anemonefish; emperor angelfish

Pages 14 and 15
Background: lionfish. Clockwise from top:
scorpionfish; larval fangtooth; inflated porcupinefish;
weedy dragonfish

Pages 16 and 17
Background: whale shark
Insets top to bottom: mouth of lamprey lined with
teeth, which bore into prey; parrotfish; adult
fangtooth

Pages 18 and 19
Background: Kelp forest
Page 18 Insets top to bottom: longnose
butterflyfish, paddlefish, sea horses
Page 19 Insets top to bottom: sawfish, deep-sea
anglerfish

Pages 20 and 21
Background: spotjaw blenny. Inset clockwise from
top left: scorpionfish eye; eyes of a lingcod with
copepod parasites

Page 22 Background: Bennett's butterflyfish.
Inset: four-spot butterflyfish
Page 23 Background: crocodilefish. Inset: eye of
stingray

Pages 24 and 25
Background: school of damselfish
Insets left to right: flashlight fish; eyes of deep-sea
hatchetfish; peacock flounder

Page 26 Background: California moray eel. Insets
top to bottom: cowfish; yellow phase of spotted
puffer; porcupinefish
Page 27 Background: deep-sea viperfish. Insets
top to bottom: deep-sea cat shark; deep-sea
anglerfish

Page 28 Background: porcupinefish. Inset: gopher
rockfish
Page 29 Background: dragon moray eel. Insets top
to bottom: frogfish; giant jawfish hiding in sand;
hammerhead shark

Pages 30
Background: anemonefish. Inset: damselfish

Page 31 Background: school of larval fish. Insets
top to bottom: batfish; anemonefish